Mbembe
Selected Poems

Mbembe
Selected Poems

Mbembe Milton Smith

BkMk Press
University of Missouri-Kansas City

Front cover design: Michael Stephens

Financial assistance for this project has been provided by the National Endowment for the Arts and by the Bernardin Fund, College of Arts and Sciences, University of Missouri-Kansas City. Second printing assistance provided by the UMKC College of Arts and Sciences Alumni Board.

Library of Congress Cataloging-in-Publication Data

Smith, Mbembe Milton, 1946-1982.
    Selected poems of Mbembe Milton Smith.

        I.   Title
        PS3569.M537824A6 1986 811'.54 85-70737
        ISBN 0-933532-50-4

Special thanks to Frank Higgins, Stanley E. Banks, and David Ray for acting as consultants to the editor in the 1986 preparation of this volume. Sincere appreciation to Samella Myers Gates for her cooperation and aid.

The poem, "a black poet leaps to his death," was first published by *The American Poetry Review* and appears here courtesy of the author, Etheridge Knight.

BkMk Press staff. For first printing: Dan Jaffe, editor-in-chief, Pat Huyett, associate editor; for second printing: Robert Stewart, editor, Ben Furnish, managing editor, Michelle Boisseau, associate editor, Susan L. Schurman, assistant managing editor, Stacey Tolbert, research assistant, Teresa Collins, editorial assistant, with thanks to Betsy Beasley, Bill Beeson, Amy Lucas, Matthew Merryman.

This book is set in Giovanni Book and Franklin Gothic Condensed.
Second printing, 2006

Some of these poems originally appeared in Mbembe Milton Smith's previous books, *To Go On, Allegory of the Bebop Walk, Playing Side Two, Consolation Prizes,* as well as the anthologies *The Next World: Poems by Third World Americans* and *The Broadside Annual,* and in a number of periodicals, including *The Kansas City Star, Mother Jones, Obsidian, Black Books Bulletin, Chariton Review, Black Scholar, Yardbird Reader, Tempo, Chouteau Review, Nimrod, Callaloo,* and *New Letters.*

For my son, Mbembe Milton Smith

My heart searches, remembering, feeling,
    researching, cataloguing thirty-five
    years,
journey of mother and son from birth, now
    converged, to death, now separate.

Having been, he is with us still.

—Samella Myers Gates

Mbembe Milton Smith (1946-1982) received his B.A. and his M.A., with an emphasis in creative writing, from the University of Missouri-Kansas City. Before his untimely death he published four books of poems: *To Go On, Allegory of the Bebop Walk, Playing Side Two,* and *Consolation Prizes.* His poems appeared widely in newspapers and magazines. Anthologies were beginning to pick up his work. He taught at Rockhurst College, Fordham University, and in the City University of New York system. The *Black American Literature Forum* said of his work, "Mbembe's poems express a hunger for a fuller life, for an affirmation of existence." *The Kansas City Star* commented, "Mbembe works with his own special problem of saying what he has to say and saying it in the authentic voice of a special culture." The literary quarterly *Northeast* summed up his work by suggesting we look for his light "on the dark waters of the bay—red flashing four: courage; white flashing one: love—you will find your way safely to harbor."

CONTENTS

INTRODUCTION

from TO GO ON

from ALLEGORY OF THE BEBOP WALK

from **PLAYING SIDE TWO**

from **CONSOLATION PRIZES**

PREVIOUSLY UNCOLLECTED POEMS

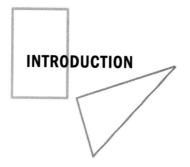

INTRODUCTION

EDITOR'S NOTE

Mbembe Milton Smith did not just leave town. He flew out of a window on the 18th floor of the YMCA building in Chicago. He fell onto a car below, shocking the bewildered driver.

Fellow writers, readers, friends, and family felt bewildered, too. Mbembe's death on September 13, 1982, could not be satisfied by a cliché explanation. It was not enough to say he was a talented and sensitive black writer who succumbed to the injustices of the world. It was insufficient to suggest that he was driven to death by prejudice, by conditions he could not correct and could no longer abide. It does not satisfy to say that a vulnerable poet living in the flame of his talent burned out because of the intensity of his inner life. After his death, I listened to the talk of the numbed, the hurt, the angered. The comments about the incredible waste of Mbembe's early death always contained a note of sadness.

There was wide agreement that he was a writer of consequence whose poems and stories had more than ordinary merit. The judgment is not sentimental. His four books of poems, *To Go On, Allegory of the Bebop Walk, Playing Side Two,* and *Consolation Prizes* attest to the achievement. In addition, Mbembe left a considerable number of short stories, at least two other poetry manuscripts, as well as experimental and unfinished work. We hope this book will help confirm his poetic stature.

To be a poet in the 1980s is almost to be an anachronism. Mbembe was a modern man, concerned with social issues, who nevertheless insisted on being a poet. Involved deeply as he was in a life-giving necessity, his suicide, like the suicide of any real artist, is a paradox almost impossible to explain or to bear.

—Dan Jaffe, 1986

THE FINALE

(Upon the occasion of Mbembe Milton Smith's death)

Right from the jump,
    let everyone understand,
    his death was not suicide,
    just his way of ending—
    after eighteen stories,
    a long triumphant poem.
Right from the jump,
    it's understood,
    his flesh is without life,
    but his words will forever
    rap to us from the pages
    to tell the story
    of how he came to the point
    of period in his life.
Right from the jump,
    Mbembe like his poetry
    pinched at the nerves
    that nagged at the black and white truth
    about us all.

—Stanley E. Banks

FOR MBEMBE
(three years after)

Now the critics can begin.
I hear a trembling out there,
a chittering, a chattering, chaffer
where there was silence
when you so needed,
came around, knocked on so many
doors. I recall your telling me
what you had already discovered—
that it was all merely a game, a *literary*
game, you said, very phony,
not what you are but who you know,
and other even more primitive
facts of the zoo. Back home, you grinned,
rocked in my rocking chair, spoke of your son,
and I had seen you, happy with him,
somehow making that old car
rock down the road, proclaim that you
and Tarik were together, the whole weekend.
So naturally I thought that you
with your immense talent, sense of humor,
blackness opaque against the false
glittering lights, would make it.
And what does that mean, making it?
That the critics can begin,
the chittering, the chattering, the trembling.

—David Ray

A BLACK POET LEAPS TO HIS DEATH
for mbembe milton smith

was it a blast to the balls dear brother
with the wind ringing in the ear
that great rush against the air
that great push
                    into the universe

you are not now alone mbembe
of the innocent eyes sadder
than a mondays rain it is i
who hear your crush of bone
            your splatter of brain
            your tear of flesh
on the cold chicago stone

                    and my october cry
when the yellow moon is ringed with blood
of children dead in the lebanese mud
            is as sharp as a kc switchblade
your pain is a slash across my throat
i feel a chill can the poet belie
the poem

            old revolutionaries never die
it is said
        they just be born again
(check chuck colson and his panther from folsom)
but you are dead
mbembe poetman in the home of the brave
the brown leaves whisper across your grave

but it must have been a rush a great gasp
                of breath
                the awesome leap to your death

o poet of the blood and bone
             of the short song
             and serious belief
i sing you release.

**—Etheridge Knight
October 1982**

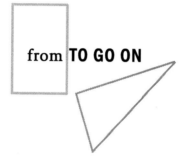

from **TO GO ON**

SURVIVAL POEM

we can slide into sleep in dead winter
in front of the pool hall
or in the alley behind the record shop
denying that we are oppressed,
awaiting the arrival of our savior
with trump cards like w.c. fields
drawing the fifth ace,
we can be corny,
relish in our own trips.
we can count the cracks in the sidewalk
scratch our asses
smile hiply at sisters
wear dashikis and drive little cars,
we can watch the greenbay packers on t.v.
or airplanes in the sky,
we can be niggers
while every breeze whispers death,
& finally perish like dinosaurs,
our skulls in showcases at the new york museum.
we can let our speech become air
& our fist soft clay.

or we can rise
up thru these filthy towns
to rule our own space.

CAUTION

when u dig what's goin' down
all that u need to know of it,
keep your eyes open with match sticks,
but don't get so strung out
you think whitey is a ghost spirit
& every niggah talking shit,
including yoself, is the black messiah.
but
know that everybody
whose front teeth smile
or make a peace sign,
ain't a guru
& everybody with a clenched fist
or a new handshake
ain't yo' brotha'.

LOVE POEM
(for Wema)

and she washed my soul
then slid off into her dreams
with a wisp of a smile on her face.
when i awakened this morning
she was gone.   no alarm;
white folks say work, we work.

HIGH

friday night I stand with spread legs
on top of the house
& look down thru the night,
thru the roof beams
into the sleeping negro skulls.
& always lurking there
is the white boy's death.   come
saturday night on the roof, i am
the blk god, Satchmo grown magnanimous
on hog maws, Muhammed Speaks
& some bush the panamanians
nurtured with gunpowder.
i shake my finger at the night,
pace the roof with my bible
clutched against my chest.
i hurl lightning at the suburbs.
then sunday morning i am there,
snow melting into house gutters,
my soul a mad man captured,
banging his head on the guilted air,
my body limp & peaceful.
the sound of billy graham
floats up from the radios
soothing me like a woman's hand.
& i am there on the roof
unable to brush my teeth
or take a shit,
wondering how i get down.

POEM FOR MY GRANDFATHER, A PREACHERMAN

grandmother told me
i should be a preacherman like you
but there are no sermons here
& she doesn't ask about church now.
i read your book for life
don't give us bibles.
give us traitors knives and rifles.
thick sole boots.   we take muscles before god,
the earth, so we can truly
see the sky, not what white folks gave us,
not this thing that cowers with the gaze
of any righteous fire, some god whose mother
kept him inside playing the piano,
while we combed the jungles
looking for people to beat up.
Africa is rising & europe's gods
leave only a monotonous survival song,
that plays on not as you wanted.
but as a concerto of kingfish niggers,
plays on in the person of rev. dr. chickenlegs,
the jesus lover with a fat hip pocket.
there is nothing left of fire or brimstone
but slick suits selling us prayers, old negroes,
who want to die in bed.   listen to their song;
"i can't sit down, i can't sit down,
my soul's so happy i can't sit down."
it's true granddad i too have drawn lots.
i take beads on the preacherman.
there are 24 years of rain washing you down
& I seldom pray.   i wear italian shoes
& know the kiss of death.
i can't sit down, i can't sit down.

PHOTOS

The funky sound of organ jazz,
a bushhead nodding to
his higher reality,
a pimp says, "run 'em around
the bar, Jack, and don't a whore
touch a drop." the smoke pushes
toward the ceiling in a thick blue
haze to escape the nigger reality.
a faggot blushes like a bitch.
a square drops a pill in a school teacher's drink.
two mod dressed brothers slap hands.
ask them and they will say
they are "joint hopping."
the white boy at the bar who dances flat footed
knows that he is "slumming."
the big butt mothers of bastard children
bounce thru the aisles trying to catch a man.
the pimps are gamin' , the whores are hustlin';
photos of the natives taken saturday night—positives
if you can get them from these negatives.
quick slick, take 'em and build.

from **ALLEGORY OF THE BEBOP WALK**

PUSHING DOPE FOR THE MAN
(in memory of Roach)

it's not so much
that i mourn you,
with Dick Haney, Tommy, you;
i'm too much the realist.

don't get me wrong; i dream.
but i distinguish between dreams & shakey schemes
that hang out on the corner near the edge.
schemes, i wrestle with,
pry their mouths,
make them tell the truth
                 if i didn't they'd throw me,
                 kick dirt in my face.
one can talk sense to them
only after they're subdued.

it wasn't just weed, Roach,
or dark glasses at midnight.
it was the way you climbed
to the top of illusions
like drugs were a beanstalk.

they found you
hands & feet bound
face down in the smell
of a project hallway,
hazard of the occupation.

i didn't mourn god's death;
i won't mourn yours.
i simply passed the corner today
& didn't see you.

THE WORLD IS A STUBBED TOE

Pick up my pen
I can write anything:
say the moon's
a round face yellow nymph,
that there's a heaven,
that I can slide down
a mile long razor blade
and not cut my ass,
that I can walk
thru a lion's cage
in a hamburger suit
and white bucks untouched,
                    fantasy shit.

but my pen stubs its toe
on this nigger reality
which is like cataracts
and old men.

ROCKING CHAIR THERAPY

in white attitude, the guard
walks past the doorless toilet, snides
"if you shake it more than three times
you ain't pissing."

Johnson in the corner has to run water
to pee, & Wilson in another,
has been here for eighteen years:
everyday's an eggshell.
Hamilton thinks he's a flying horse;
strapping him to the bed
slows his airscape gallop.

somehow they get it into our rocky heads
madness is a crime & more.

i sit in my rocker frisking myself,
my mind spread eagled
'gainst a wall in a dark psychic alley,
i shake myself down.

MORAL TO MY MADNESS

weed & speed wedge my sleep.
at 3 A.M.,
my mind turns over—
a man whose clothes are on fire.

week, speed—
eternal delusions,
quick starts that promise
                                    stroke
                                          or heart attack.
days:
     crowds shrill at me,
nights:
     a man in a trenchcoat
     waits behind the door.

madness passes in and out of me
in cycles, sure as breath.

so they fix me up
with prolyxin and thorazine;
send me out again.

but in revolution I'd be regal;
when the people came
to storm the institution gates,
I'd step into the sunlight, blinking,
more lovely than the Marquis de Sade.

ANCESTRY AS REALITY
(for Tarik)

it was a friend saying
"look man, divorce
doesn't make bad children,
bad parents do," that stuck
in the weak side of better judgment.
so i pushed against the cycle—poor, black
    fatherless—
to see if it would break.
it haunts me
with apparitions of my own father
his eyes beady as a pair of craps,
a bottle of cheap gin
on his kitchen table,
him, way off in Omaha.

when the measles, the whooping coughs,
father's day get you, when at school
the skilled surgeons cut the good black stuff
from your head, i may not be there.
but you'll have the weekends, summers,
me pleading—"Tarik, daddy loves you,
do you love daddy?" weekends
when I rub you 'gainst my hairless chest
& try to convince you
i wanted to be a man.

FOR TARIK

it will be important to you,
that on a january night
we warmed ourselves with Manischewitz
& stacked the records. Doug Carn's
"Infant Eyes" played all night
as we danced our passion
across the bedroom.
still, it was mindless movement,
the wrong time of the month
that brought you light.

in my father's house there were two bedrooms,
in his father's house there were two.
in my house there is room, son.
i go to prepare a place.

THE OLD WOMAN IN THE GREEN
   HOUSE ON THE CORNER

even the crudest cynics
don't curse or talk loud
in her presence.
if i light a cigarette
there's a terrible irony
in the matching color of her wig,
the smoke curling upward.
                    she has no vices,
drinks coffee only to stay awake in church.

it's senseless to tell her
that death is more than an idea,
that there are no neatly trimmed hedges in heaven,
nor roses, nor air, that her false teeth will not
be in the cup on the night stand.

her life is 83 years of upright chairs,
Sunday chicken, Sunday china, walking
the living perpendicular.

the only evidence of a crack in her faith
is a nervous thumb,
tapping like a metronome
even when she prays.

ALLEGORY OF THE BEBOP WALK

there are uncharted places
like Overland Park, Kansas, or Greenwich, Conn.
where they'd lock the back door
if they heard black power was coming
'cause black folk wouldn't dare
come 'round the front.

in these territories
our faces are long survivors
from days of stingy brims
and pointed shoes, or Rochester, Beaulah and co.,
days of a million changes
until a bebop walk broke down before the logic
of a stiff gait, logic that is visa
into white and light domains.

now there's no way back
and no convenient solace within miles
just a vast unfamiliar turf
and a few of us looking in vain
for Afro-Sheen in the suburban drugstore.

A POEM TO THRILL THE NAACP OR
A BLACK FAMILY MOVES TO THE SUBURBS

he was black, yes,
but his plans were not nigger.
so when they stole his car battery again
he and wife
and little Tamara
and little Martin Luther moved
out there,
left behind the black folk next door
who think the mailman
cases their house,
who sit 'til the charging sun rises,
with ready shotgun
and eye the young dudes
'cross the street,
waxing old Cadillacs
under the street lamp
'til they shine new rich, hip
for city showboating,
just right for jittabugs low-riding,
leaning on their pimp stool arm rest,
polishing their sunglasses
with "Posh Puffs," breathing their gangster air,
'til the night turns whoreless.
they got tired
and moved out there
left a naked black doll in the dust
where the couch had been,
left the bars on the windows
of the rented apartment,
gave his last pair of lime pants
to Good Will,
went devouring their way
into middle america,
lean and mean,
half piranha, half education.

THE PRESIDENT IS ON THE EVENING NEWS

12 years old,
i could do the hand jive,
hurdle a picket fence,
hum one thru the hoop
& kick the nets back up.
track stars were gods,
basketball players lords.
money was a hole in my pocket.
someday i'd be a god.

now all my dreams are knee deep in mud.
i'm nostalgic about a nightmare
where i get 60 years to sink one
in a big basketball goal in the sky.

& god up there,
he think he pretty,
stands in the mirror—
wonders which gray suit to wear,
thinks of being president,
trickling down dollars
from a hole he's poked in heaven,
thinks of clouded speeches, limousine
and waving smiles.

the hurdlers
all got cinders in their eyes
from too many gray nights
slumped in soft chairs
like a limp conveyor belt
or an empty mail bag,
watching the evening news
& the president
doing the hand jive
from a limousine
in the clouds.

THE SUN'S A LIAR

my grandmother said solemly,
"you know your Uncle Clarence passed?"

as i measured for the right words,
she broke the chasm with,
"i wonder if you
would paint my porch sometime?"

so we stick our finitude
under a church pew
like chewing gum
say the sun's a liar
and throw rocks at it,
or talk intrepid, 'til we go mad

or 'til death rips us away raw
like drafts from a poet's notebook.

SOMETHING ELSE THEY SAY

is that jazz is dead
but i want to tell you
that in a wooden loft in chicago
Archie Shepp gave artificial respiration
to a carcass.

no gimmicks,
no electricity coming from his sax,
just the naked instrument
that hung limp
from a thin red tie.

Shepp was dressed in a 1950 cotton suit,
faded and slick like rat fur.
when the sounds got good to him
he took off his coat
and turned to the band.
his hip pocket was snagged from years
of dragging a gin bottle.

as he blew
the words of critics flaked away.
the music they say is dead
was so alive, it sweated.

OTHER BOOKS BY THE AUTHOR

"My poetry is poetry of the proletariat
by the proletariat and for the bourgeoisie."
Melvin B. Tolson

look, bored middle mania
this is all the bleeding
i can do. and even if i wrote
a novel, long spills that singed
your eyes, you'd say somebody
else said it better.

i don't find it childish
that scissors cut paper
or the least bit amusing
that i'm driven to write this stuff;
rage deterred
like a still life
of an apple
      and
         a hatchet.

from **PLAYING SIDE TWO**

YOUR SELF-FULFILLING HISTORY

Actually poems are not my style,
not the way i comb my hair
or walk along the street,
not the way i sit
or hold my woman.
there is a thumb twiddling in them
that disgusts me,
a form to them that peeves,
a content that doesn't say enough.
if you want to know the truth
i could care less about a period
at the end of this sentence
for i have no desire to stop you here. . .
the idea is to punctuate reality,
to make the real stuff of life
a work of art. . .

FOR FRANK HIGGINS, POET
(who said he was the great white hope
when I said, "I am a black poet")

you laugh, man,
but it's no joke.
we're fighting
sure as shit.
if not each other
then it's the world & us.
haven't you seen the fight card,
the names on the marquee?
it's always the poet against the world.

the world's got an iron jaw
& a killer instinct.
best we can hope for
is cauliflowered ears,
a lumpy nose,
welts above the eyes.

but if you want beauty
you've got to fight for it.

already they've got me punch drunk,
coming out my corner
when there's no bell.

THE ROMANCE OF COMING TO NEW YORK

romance, unlike a tree, never roots
rather scorns the earth,
reaches always for the sun.
off to war at 17,
tho maimed & crippled
comes crying revolt at 21,
                    should it return at all.

still untamed,
it loves & leaps
but never limps.
            an airy idea of history
made solely with the songs of heart.

so i came, a grain of sand
in my palm, mortar enough
to slay the skyscrapers,
remake New York, New York.

the subway simply
rides over me
& only the prostitute
licks her lips like love.

nevertheless i came
for the sentimental journey
"A" train to Harlem
where long dreamy songs get off
& encore before naked reality.

i came
to phallic Manhattan
a horny pair of shoes in the store window,

the women on the subways
clasping their purses tightly
concealing the miscellaneous
makeups & esoterics.

New York, New York
infirmary of the ego,
blind city that drags my people behind it
like a lump of seeing-eye dog.
New York, New York
property, pathos & felled romance.

MOOD POEM
Frank's Bar & Restaurant (Kansas City)

The menu entries are
catfish
chicken
chitterlings (in season)
candied yams
collard greens

in this restaurant
black men ensconce
& cross their legs
into the aisles.
there's a certain kingliness
revealed in nylon ankle socks
distinguished shaving scars,
trimmed mustaches, spiced cologne smells
& five hundred dollar diamond rings.

the ladies are ladies
only linen napkins will do,
a bit of cream in their coffee.

soft sin & warmth,
laughter, food, propriety—

this is where i'm coming from,

from vegetables, meat,
from sturdy green life.
this is where i go
to order fried chicken
or just sit
& listen to King Pleasure
on the juke box.

GOD, THE MASK
New York 1979
The Reign of Jimmy Carter

you've got it all wrong, America
god will refuse to slap you on the back
& say, "way to go." he will not
throw down a few beers with you
at the corner bar. he will not go
to the football game. he is a delicate
turn in events, weakness in every strength.
when you grab at him with your meaty hands,
your heavy girders reaching skyward,
your robust façade, opposites will break you.
anything godly displays itself so gently,
proposes so many futures, subtle as illusion,
that to find god absent in them
will not undo the scheme.
everything will be in order,
try as you will to impose another will—
the end, fine delicate things, old subtle twists,
strange tanglings in history's hair
in the wind & rain will sneak up on you,
to say peek-a-boo in the end.
god is a mask.
he does not believe in anything gaudy or corny.
he does not wear red, white, or blue. . .

BUCKS

at 3:30 A.M.
on the subway uptown
a young brother, 17 or 18, says
"you got a cigarette, man?"
his hand is bandaged,
his hat pulled down
around the left eye,
cocked ace, deuce,
his collar turned up 'gainst the hawk.
i've known him all my life,
the cold cities, elemental graces,
the sordid elements that stir us.

when i give him a smoke.   i nod to him,
                           slow,
                           deliberate.
'i agree to disagree' cements the gesture,
but i dare not hazard a light.

mostly i treat this kid as city hall treats him,
no matter that he's a child,
no kid's gloves, no sappy emotions
when a huff of ego, a clumsy finger
could send the world up in puff.

same way, i could be some kid's big brother,
same way, i could be seven random lines
                       in the morning paper.

NOSTALGIA OF THE MUD
(for Etheridge Knight)

you remind me of my father—
the pain somehow aesthetic,
the way they've strung you out
over a religion

    that skips Sunday,
turns up red-eyed
'bout 2 o'clock Monday afternoon.

there's a jazz riff, a waywardness
at the core of your Karma,
reminds me of the time
the family was walking from church
& we dug my old man
in the alley drinking wine.

must be we inherit red eyes,
our folk hugged against ghetto walls
bent by so much dark blue living.

give me the bottle too.
hope this poem kills the poison
off the wine we've uncapped
but if not, drink up, pass the grapes 'round.

PAIN-KILLER

it
always
seemed
to
me
that
agnosticism
was mostly
agony.
you question.
i question you.
why punish yourself?
when my tooth got rotten
i pulled it out roots & all.
i've done the same with throbbing gods.

LONELY WOMEN

we come up thru these cities
not really noticing
winos in front of the liquor store,
our fathers' small waning wills.

it would be a simple test
taking them to the basket
then falling away
with a good jump shot,
their eyes burning.
we taunted white boys
with our strident walks,
our humorous hipness.

now
after war, after wide-eyed wonder
there's only dope, the deaths, the dying,
our women at the bar staring into the mirror.

THE SOCIAL CONTRACT

On Braniff 727 over Kansas
the man next to the window
from South Dakota,
going to see his son in Texas says,
"how far up, ya think,
a mile, mile & a half?"
down below, the muddy Missouri
wriggling along Kansas.
he's a farmer, knows river,
believes in territorial imperatives,
has grinned at me
to show he won't use his teeth
     as a weapon,
has shaken my hand—
nothing hidden in his.
"You're a gentleman, buddy," he says,
as i hand him change from the hostess.
he sips his drink—
"You're a gentleman," he says,
spraying my brown hand with apple spit.
he knows by now where i'm from,
what i do, he thinks he knows
where i'm going.
but i've known him all my life,
the way his socks droop,
the way the dirt won't wash
from beneath his fingernails,
the way he drinks & drools.
when he says he's got nothing
against my people, i knew he'd say it.
& i know poverty keeps him honest;
he can't afford to oppress.
it's the man in the aisle seat

reading an application
for a Cadillac dealership,
his gold cufflinks,
his diamond pinky,
his dark blue suit.
i imagine him in his office
ten floors up, picking up the phone
& dialing my death.

THE BLACK MESSIAH

O' god
i saw your fiery light thru my bedroom window
the burning cross, the whole prophecy
stretched out before me like a row
of day old donuts in the bakery.
but i was drunk on cheap wine
& the smell of acapulco gold
was on my fingers.
so i mistook your light
for the streetlight in my eyes,
for a dream the morning paper wouldn't print.
"lead them," he said & not even a manual
on guerilla warfare magically appeared.
so while the night waxed & waned
outside my bedroom
i waited narcotized,
for an unambiguous sign.

in the morning i rose from bed
with an unsaintly hangover
to go into the crowded ghetto streets
& announce to them by my silence
that i couldn't save them.

YOU'VE GOT TO LEARN
THE WHITE MAN'S GAME
for Taylor

the 5th black law student
at the university of missouri
squats, away from the grandstands,
at the top of a hill
whistling a jazz tune.
the football game bored him to murder,
the lions & christians, the christians, esp.
the gladiators, the whole show
with red-necks in little red caps
shouting, "go, go, Nebraska, big red."
he could tell 'em 'bout red.
he dreamed in that color.

take it up the sideline, cut back,
down the middle, shove it
down their throats
stand at home plate smiling,
connect with a right & dance
above their slumped bodies.
he dreamed in red, blood red.
"But Not For Me" he whistled consciously
as he sat on his haunches
at the top of the hill
& let the cold whip
the back of his neck.
he would play the game,
be a cool honcho,
play the game.

he would squat
at the top of the hill
& maybe convince himself
it's all sport.

THE KU KLUX KLAN

they die slow
like the cowboy
at high noon
who will not go down
under the bright hot sun
but falls, rises, falls,
stumbles backwards thru the pgs. of history,
hangs on, hangs on, until his legs
give out
& he tumbles,
irrecoverable,
forever.

they
die
slow
like
inch-worms
in molasses,
with 22 supporters in New Jersey
they
run
for
president,
crawl
from
under
rocks
in Alabama,
with rifles,
they surface,
to defame
the name
of our great leaders,

make us feel guilty
by mere fact
of association—
we were on the planet   earth
at the same time
as
they.

dogged—
their ignorance,
dipping snuff,
chewing tobacco.
they make of cigars
a profaneness,
give beer
an aura of racism.
i refuse to be more detailed
to name the one next door—
they should be as invisible ink
something in them of themselves
that removes them from historical reference.

let it be assumed of them forever
what is so often wrongly
assumed of the mass.
in this case, it is right.

they were ignorant, mediocre,
cowardly, wrongheaded, stubborn, small—
they never existed.

HAWKER

there's another world
2 blocks from the university.
you make your mark here
with raw survival skills.
the streets, an education.
the old buildings, design
of slick politicians
& redlining bankers.
it could be the lower east side,
anywhere, people like us live.
what heat Con Edison doesn't supply
                the cops will.
the system, a shadowy detective.
each day the job of eluding it,
step around or beyond it cautiously.

morning now, the dreams rise up
like steam from the coffee cups
of the owners along Park Avenue.
the hawker puts on the stiff socks,
the dirty jeans, the sneakers,
an old army jacket.   he's a veteran
of the streets.   13 degrees today,
wind chill makes it zero.
        no gloves, no hat, he will huddle
in the doorways 'til early the next morning
beckoning for us.   "loose joints, brother,
something for the head today, my man?"

PLAYING SIDE TWO

a dark spirit who never rejoices
who is driven to his desk by the hell in hello,
who would always play side two of the record,
would take you down the back alleys
& side streets of imagination.

still i point up the strife & striving,
how everything John Coltrane played—
always the other side—
how life is not a perfect performance.

in all those joyous moments
an incessant blues solo,
some vital lie to be exposed, underscored:
first orgasm, that homerun.
first time you saw the sea,
children's smiles & our loves
& that breeze of a summer night,
those new shoes that autumn—
                    singular performances.

but the flip side of this,
my favorite things becomes a weeping—
the club owners just offstage, side two—
the smile now upside down,
some flaw needs correction
& the children
              so perfectly beautiful
all the more this contrast,
the valley, its shadow,
a funeral dirge in abstract,
so that even a distilled loveliness
portends a recurring scream,
an anger made melodious.

i am a brooding spirit.
i will not forgive life.
& i will not let the living forget.
there is little time for rejoicing.
hear that riff.   am i out of tune?
no, it's the world.

again & again & again it must be made right
& just & right.

again & again an art climbing the stairs
to retaliate against muzak & murder.

from **CONSOLATION PRIZES**

INVOCATION & INVITATION
(for Marion Brown, jazz saxophonist)

the linguist would never understand,
our very beings, this prayer
you make of water & of light,
prayer, without category,
our flesh some clay,
our feet sunk in it,
eyes intoning Orion.

i am lost herein
for the logic of definition,
am lost for category, for language itself,
am nameless in the face
of your haunting evocations.

erase it all, Marion,
these silly words without music,
riddle us, renew us,
reshape us,
as irredentists & as seers.

O' mysterious contrition & expansion,
make an act of love.
O' breath & lungs, approach, retreat,
god takes off her clothes for us
& is musical.

let us have ten minutes
of hallowed silence.

POLICE SKETCH ARTIST
(from a Village Voice *article)*

something like me.
didn't study too hard in college,
maybe didn't go,
drifted into the job.

now he sits at his desk
turning pages in old mug-shot books,
a chin here, a nose there,
lots of big lips.

"we try for something broad," he says.
"that is, if you see anybody
who looks like this, let us know."

most of his drawings
look like people in my family.

AFRICAN-AMERICAN

a particularly peculiar predicament,
swimming two ways at the same time,
exalting the past, suffering the present,
interrogating the future,
one face in a commercial,
two of us in a cowboy flick,
jazz musician blowing classical music
in a hole-in-a-wall.
we, here, splitting the language,
praying to gargoyles, ancestors
& linear time.

VOICES

Upstate New York,
Summer, 1980

tonight
a long way from that corner
along the Kansas City strip
& further still in mind,
17 years old, with purple pants
with moonlight/streetlight
like a spotlight
with jazz funk whining
from the parading radios
of slick cars in pass & revue:
that as image, dim now,
me among a gang of Hollywood jittabugs,
their flitting sounds, Scooby Doo
or Money Dog playing the dozens.
it's all gone now, the way
the breeze tonight floats away,
& you can't say to breezes
that you don't play the dozens
& you can't talk
about a breeze's moma.
she don't speak your language.
she only speaks in whispers,
in disquieting strange tongues
'bout all you've lost
& all that's dead & gone.

THE FORM OF CITY NIGHTS

a little lounge
next to a bar-b-que joint
we gathered at the bar
looking into the mirror,
always mirrors,
on a wall above, a mural,
    black folks,
    men in shiny suits,
    women in hot oranges,
    long faces, teeth, broad noses,
    a trumpet player with slim fingers.
somehow this mural
was as real to me as the people—
watching myself doing what i was doing,
there & not there in the smoke & talk
"Hey baby! My man, what's happenin?"
"Hey man, hey baby."
into the small hours of the night.

outside the street lights glared,
the neon signs flashed,
prostitutes & pimps stood in shadows.

there was this black cat, too,
used to chase away the dogs.

KISS/KILL AT BREAKFAST

i refuse you
the words you want
because my memory startles
at your easy universalities.
we know we're here over bagels & coffee,
that the sun shines
thru the kitchen window
& that's nearly all we know
of what's to come of this.

what if the Arabs make a bold move
with their rook & half your genealogy
goes up in smoke & stars.
all this puzzles me & too,
this moment you would build castles with
seems so much like sand.
as much as love
the sunlight on your cheeks
conjures up slave ships,
the ocean green of your eyes, an anger
subdued so well of late,
but certainly still there.

these things don't come loose
from moorings easily—
(Malcolm X, doo wop, hog maws, gospel music)
can you catch all of me
if i fall?

what i am. what the world will be,
walks ahead of us.
& this moment
could so easily move
right thru the opposition of itself
heading beyond us both to god knows where.

NAACP URGING REVIEW
BY CIVILIANS OF POLICE ACTS
New York Times,
Monday, Jan. 14, 1980

the basketball game is over.
Carver High beat Booker Washington,
72 to 53, going away at the buzzer.
the newspapermen will write up
how it was hardly a contest.
after all, Carver's center
is nearly 7 feet, hands like hams,
can dribble behind the back,
going full speed
on the downcourt break.
two weeks ago against Central
he shattered the backboard
trying to slap one down,
then loped back to the other end
like a big giraffe,

well, now he's coming up
from the locker room.
that cute little cheerleader, Linda Brown,
is waiting with a big hug & kiss.
& a few blocks away
Sergeant Shrivers
is strapping on his holster.
he's been practicing all day
with silhouettes...
          the boys around the precinct
call them "running nigger targets."

DUENDE

the phone
          rings:
my brother
          who left yesterday
on his way to California
picked up a hitchhiker
who hit the guardrail,
turned the car over three times,
then walked away from it
shaking his woozy, negligent head.

when i heard your neck was broken, Ray,
i could only think of saltine crackers,
the church, with the preacher
extending his arms, the ushers
passing the wine,
then i thought of getting drunk.

now on the highway
going to your bedside
death seems a sacrament without ceremony.

2

rabbit, in the light beams,
run over up ahead,
which Mac truck driver
stopped to have his pie & coffee,
took his bennies
at just the right time
to be on time for your death?
damn, how the insects

fly against the windshield,
how the headlights fade
along the highway.
damn, now i'm thinking
of a snowflake on a hamburger grill.
God, how this poem simply ends.

FABLE OF WATERGATE
(looking back)

one came in the window,
two slipped out the door,
one called a friend
from across the street in the bar,
three drove away,
four appeared on t.v.,
two hid in the bushes,
one ran down the fire escape,
one walked thru the revolving door,
three went out of town on business,
one took it off his taxes,
seven pulled their hats over their eyes,
twelve wrote books,
one put on a judge's robe
& hid in the closet,
two pardoned three of them,
six went on a skiing trip
& shook hands with another four.

PARTY

no use
standing
by the cheese & crackers.
the world is alarm enough
                    to wake me:
if the bloodshot sun won't
then nothing will.
but tonight those dancing hips
need dancing hips, those painted lips
need smearing.
even the full moon would be dull
when compared to the gleam
in that brownskin's eyes.

PREVIOUSLY UNCOLLECTED POEMS

THE LIFE OF THE 40 HOUR WEEK

monday   friday
    straight ahead
no glancing to the right
& especially not to the
  left.
      you are a part.
      do your part.
screw that nut on tight
so this damn thing will run.
stand there. hold this. lift that weight.
teach those children not to think.
things must go on, must go on.
there are higher purposes than your pleasure.
our convictions need your muscle.
there are prophets to prove wrong,
dissenters to control, freedoms to restrain.
what are you anyway? some kind of nut?
      a philosopher? a dreamer?
step forward, please.
      step forward, please.

HOUR OF NEED:
OUTER & INNER SANCTUARY

i could sit here forever
browsing in *Family Circle* magazines,
contemplating the pen & ink drawing
of the Empire State building,
the other of the tree & river.
forever, i could luxuriate
in the sensate blue carpet
& the leather chairs.
there is, there must be
hidden meaning in the coat rack.
everything has been thought thru here.
nothing to disturb me,
            an occasional taxi maybe,
but the muzak in the walls
takes care of that.
we are high above ground,
the place where heaven is,
just as guaranteed by the t.v. commercials,

in the inner office, he is stirring,
            preparing his text,
a little Freud, a little pragmatism
            will convince me
that things won't change this year.
i should go along to get along
& keep the capsules for restlessness & outrage
on the third shelf of the medicine cabinet.
he is right & so exorcised,
            cleansed to specification,
strapped into the Edsel of life,
marveling at the full refrigerator,

everything becomes a shrug.
time is up
45 minutes is an hour

"get out there & lock horns with them," he says,
rubbing his hands together briskly,
something like a football coach about to pray.
we shake on it, quickly—
his tepid grasp is a blessing.
i will die in bed.   & so he turns
to reenter his sanctuary where it smells
of aromatic tobacco & appointment books

& i take the elevator down,
new & normal.

CONSPIRACY

paid for being this & that,
the counsel & conscience,
paid for forcing truth,
into a single bank account,
they swear to anything,
report both sides,
like intermittent rain
as long as it pays.

at testimonial, they extol each other,
Mr. A & Mr. B
Mr. B & Mr. A
who would usurp the alphabet
for private gain,
who from adjoining suites
roast & toast each other
& laugh
& laugh
high above the prisons & snares
of their amazing summations & half-truths.

they go separately together.
together, they are never wrong.

ROCK OF AGES
(thinking of Alberta King)

we are used
to old folks
dying
their downhill lives
& used
to old folks
living on & on
rocking,
snuff
in their mouths,
rubbing their knees
with knotted knuckles,
telling stories centuries old.

sometimes with them
defiance grows round & patient,
jocular as greens in the pot
on the stove.

slowly it boils.

& proverbs
passed to us in youth
strike again & again
as we listen at the core.

their words speak & speak,
resound, resound.

she was in church.

the moneychangers' agent
fired bullets into her prayer.

now,
now
you remember.

ON THE SUNNY SIDE OF THE STREET

there's a fiftyish looking black man
with one leg & one eyed
outside the public housing office downtown
who soils our lives everyday.
in the morning
his hair is matted,
he has ash around his mouth like pus.
he wears an army shirt
pockmarked with cigarette burns,
the cigarette, constant,
jingling from the side of this mouth.
everyday he's in his wheelchair there,
smoking, coughing up vile sexual insults
& spitting them at white girls walking by.
they are secretaries, career girls
at city hall across the street
part-time models, some.
& the one leg, one eyed black man
is the bane of them all.
at workday's end
he's still there
& has sunned most of the day
except the security guard
wheels him over the doorstep for lunch.
the white girls hustle past
sweet spring evenings
in the sweet years of their lives.
sometimes the wind catches their dresses
& exposes spirited stockinged legs.
in their worst image of themselves,
when the boss has ridden them all day,
when they feel like
sticking their heads in a toilet
because the tall slender look is in,

because city administration
is a mass of maddening papers,
even on their worst days their spirits giggle.
& knowing this the one leg, one eyed black man
accuses them with his good eye
& his insults.
some cross the street,
others glance at him & glance away,
then they step around him briskly
i step around him too, briskly, briskly
as does the personnel officer,
the administrative assistant.
every evening, cross the street
step around the one leg, one eyed black man.
he's like dog shit on the street
he makes us feel so dirty.

THE BROKEN CHURCH WINDOW

from the broken church window
the view, a dream vomiting up
its chug of rotgut wine,
a child with distended belly
walks on water & all my flowers
are wilted & dead.
you see, this woman & me, i mean part of me,
like she's got a halo & we're sitting
at a sidewalk restaurant
eating celery & snowflakes
& everything is hard to explain.

from the broken church window,
a long distance between me
       & my feelings about iron ore,
a gaping hole between one chair
& the next.

behind the broken church window
i'm making love to a beautiful woman
by standing on tiptoes
& children are watching
as helium balloons float away.

from the broken church window
i'm resigned to it,
this time i'll never find another job
because a Chinese CIA agent fingerprinted me
& sent my B.A. degree to Nigeria
to show the Africans that self-help works.

from the broken church window
my mind spins out in endless webs
& sometimes i bolt upright in my bed
wondering if our lord & saviour
will be coming to clean the garbage
off the streets at dawn.

CONFESSION: THE HARLEM RENAISSANCE

"I was Brother Taboo-with-whom-all-things-are-possible."
Ralph Ellison

she was white
as the window shades
we kept drawn.
& tho i wasn't expected to sing
(since times have changed)
i felt good
& sang anyway
& flexed my muscles too,
mindless of Paul Robeson or Jack Johnson.
she wasn't bad tho,
given myth
& the experimental way
i retested the hypothesis.
no, they aren't inherently colder or hotter.
no, black into white
doesn't equal some weird kind of disease,
simply that the chemistry was right that night,
or day, as was the case.
no, it doesn't prove manhood,
doesn't even promise proof of manhood.
there was tho, a creeping superiority
in her talk, compounded
by the hairs on her breast,
at least twelve long blond strands
when we let the sun in.
yet even that was undermined
by crying spells
& submission to strongly posed argument,
blunt rhetoricals,
like, "are you what they call
poor white trash?"
that was mean of me,
tho so much like me.

all in all it was absurdly normal.

POEM FOR HENRY GILES ON DEATH ROW IN ARKANSAS

Henry Giles with an I.Q. of 59,
Henry Giles on death row
at Cummins Prison Farm,
Stuttering and mostly deaf
Henry Giles against the wall
is no mockingbird,
no symbolism,
no subtlety,
but iron cooked goose
without thought of flight
or sense enough to fly
or wings with which.

against the wall
without even knowledge
of the wall or beyond.

"Eh" says Henry Giles
to ascension into heaven.
"Eh" says Henry Giles
to society and to the booming
voice of god
"Wha, wha, what he say?"
Henry Giles says
who can only understand
by analogy that to be
electrocuted is barbecued
in the language of the law.

Henry Giles, the horror
in a pregnant black woman's
stomach that keeps her up
all night for even normal
is nigger,

is inferior,
is every trip of the train
a struggle to survive.

Henry Giles who they said
had free will to kill,
who had never been free,
who had no will,
stumbled into the world
and fell on his face.

Henry Giles could get rich
if the Shockley plan
is ever given credence;
$1,000 for every point
below the I.Q. of 100.
$41,000 for Henry Giles
and the choice
to spend the rest of his life
in the nuthouse, washing
walls, being kicked in the pants,
being told to shower and pee
and take his medicine.

Henry Giles
who they might barbecue
if we don't raise our voices.

AMERICAN HISTORY, POPULAR VERSION

George Washington is crossing the Delaware
on a beaten horse.
Alexander Hamilton is dying in a frilly shirt
with a pale woman kneeling over him.
Thomas Jefferson is sitting in dim light
scribbling on a thin parchment.
two men with white wigs are shaking hands
on the porch of a mansion.
Paul Revere's hair is streaming in the wind.
a frail woman is standing at a window.
another is seated at a bureau
brushing her long brown hair.
Abraham Lincoln is walking a dirt road
his big bony wrists sticking from his coat sleeves.

we're down in there somewhere,
a mule with a hard row to hoe,
a pair of black hands
clutching the whitest cotton,
down there grinning
or just seething in silence,
our eyes rolling around in our heads,
our tongues beseeching the burning yellow sun.

GOOD MORNING

you could leave your crib
'bout 6 o'clock in the morning
cause you a poet of the people
& want a cup of coffee
& ole Willie be up
& on the corner drinking port,
talking 'bout "been down so long
rising ain't eben crossed my mind."
& you'd pass him by
but the whore be on the street
waving at the cars, ain't been to sleep.
& the woman in the subway booth
be getting an education for her children,
40 hrs. a week, double overtime on holidays
& she'd be up. you ain't got to check—she's there.
& Bertha be going out to Westchester
in her white uniform to get breakfast
for them white folks. ain't never been
no black revolution way she sees it.
& Sam have his lunch pail, heading on in.
& the one after your heart be standing
at the bus stop with her briefcase
& her afro trimmed, looking like she wanted
you with her last night, got her mouth poked out,
looking proud enough to make things fun.
she got the red sun in her eyes
& the cool morning playing
round the hem of her cotton skirt.

you be feeling like praying
like saying "good morning, good morning."
man, this is what we mean
when we say "the black aesthetic."
we a people getting up.

A DAY OF TRYING TO MAKE
PARADOXES GO AWAY

as a child, it didn't make sense—
make my bed, to get in it again at night?
why does the early bird get the worm?
'cause the worm got up too late.

question!
you'll find the answer
has been wronged from the start.
i.e. Is, the world fucked up?
answer—love.

today, brotherman stopped me on the street.
"look man, whitey is your natural enemy," he said.
he was clearly wrong, natural?
not white on black, black on white.
he'd righted the answer 'til he'd wronged it.
"what you gon' tell your children
when they ask why they slaves?" he said.
"revolution is the only way, brotha'
& revolution is bloodshed."
& on & on he went, offering me a lifestyle
that said simply meant death.
but i was 6 thoughts deeper,
five philosophies beyond,
hells he hadn't imagined.
last count there were 2 dozen issues
worth dying for. i'm obviously fit to live.
as for my kid—right now, i make him
make his bed religiously.
as for bloodshed, i'm already bleeding.

6 o'clock this evening
i got in bed & pulled myself
into the fetal position.

what is love?
obviously, the answer is love.
& that, my man, is an answer
wronged & wronged again,
a question that unfolds forever, or should
like a joyful scream from the center of a woman,
the center of a flower or the sun
& everything that gives or lives.

DOING MANHOURS IN THE MADHOUSE

He was almost trite,
like a happy face
at the pancake house—
cherries for the eyes & nose,
a pineapple for the mouth
of the pancake happy face.
he was human.
if you scratched him, he'd bleed.
but then in a way, he wouldn't.
he could stand at the window
looking thru the iron bars
& watch the sun go down
feeling neither hurt nor loss.
he'd pass you in the corridor
& say, "top of the morning to you,"
as if he was white
& you'd greeted him
in the streets of Boston, 1939.
he acted like he was always on his way
to buy the morning paper—
that good-day-to-invest mentality.
"What's happening, Jones," i'd say
"Aw, time aint' long as it has been,
ain't short as it's gon' get," he'd say.
& if i quizzed him,
"Why so happy, Jones?"
he'd say, "You know brotha,
some of these cats 'round here moping
'cause they doin' time,
but I ain't doin' time.
I'm a man; and I'm doin' manhours."

DAVID, THE MANCHILD

14 years old,
dipped onto the ward
with his hand casted,
had broken another kid's nose
on the minimum security side.
they made him shower,
scrubbed his hair for lice,
took away his shoes & shoestrings
& gave him white terry cloth cat slippers.
he sat & rocked & sobbed, long & deep.
"what's the matter?" i said.
"ain't good for a kid
to be with all these men,
ain't good," he said, sniffling.

the men leered at him.
showed brown tobacco teeth.
"i gotta be a man now," he said
& timidly asked for a cigarette.

it was all the Bar Mitzvah he'd ever have.

when he got his hand out of cast,
he giggled, gave clenched fist salutes.
        easy smiles broke from his mouth
like wave on wave of ghetto classrooms
full of mischief & insurrectionary anger.

BENNY, 18 YEARS

"You don't understand.
it's not the long floating blues
of Coltrane that I speak of,
or B.B. King
saying, 'nobody loves me but my moma
and she could be jiving too.'
those are noble states of mind,
triumph thru art, ascendancy,
and finally, blues not final at all,
just a way station with a way out.
blues like that come and go, come and go
but keep going on.
the blues i'm talking
will not be twisted by song,
will not sing; they're darker still.
i mean not my woman gone,
the guitar on the bed,
but not the will to pick it up.
the blues i'm talking is the guitar gone too.
the blues i'm talking is the bed gone.
the blues i'm talking are darker still,
darker still."

he would have said this
if blues singers were ever analytical,
if the blues were analytical
or if he'd been.
instead he just huddles there
on the bughouse steps,
near the gymnasium
shaking his head,
left to right, right to left,
moaning once in a while.

LACE

the white patients
consoled themselves
by saying Lace was seeing things.
he saw nightmares
in their pale indoor skins.
his hands were quick hallucinations
when they took their eyes off him.
they'd be playing rummy,
going on about war
& Korean girls with vaginas
that slit sideways.
"Jeez", some small town nuthouse
corporal who'd killed his wife
& children would say.
then his head would snap
from a left jab
& Lace be standing over him
serene as a fisherman at midnight.
never more than one punch at a time,
wouldn't say nothing to nobody,
black or white
just hallucinated rage on white folks.

Johnson, who'd been locked up 20 years
("seen 'em come and go,")
said Lace wasn't never gon' get out.

COUNTRY BOY

he did several things
absolutely essential to survival
in such a place: smoked a corncob,
chewed tobacco, patted his size 15 shoes
to hillbilly music, said "By God" with
a wonderful twang.   he was one of them.

6 feet, 6 inches, 270, 280—
tho a long scar down to his forehead
had tamed him, they still feared him
except one little guard with a Napoleonic complex
would kick him in the rear, every chance he got,
exalting in the wonders of modern medicine.

i thought i'd heard all the stories.

    even tho after his 29 years there
    i could still picture him
    tossing hay over his shoulder,
    sitting in front of the store
    whittling away, tho i could hear
    the cows mooing in his speech,

to think that with all those rapists & murderers
from the big city, they'd lobotomized him
for cattle rustling. it was more than absurd.
it was crazy.

RALPH

You've seen old men,
all day in the park,
the checker game—
each studied move
approach—avoidance
to the refusal of death.
they wait at noon for bedtime.
this one was like that.
he was 37 years old—
had acquired a quiet madness.
he had split a man's head
with a meat cleaver
& said god told him to.
he would rock his chair once
& then not again for an hour.
but the misery was in the marrow all day.
he had no dreams
& perhaps no nightmares.
'bout 9:30
he'd anticipate the guard
unlocking the rooms for bed at 10:00.
he'd lean over & say to me,
"getting short to get long all over again."

THE DOCTOR'S GLASSES

the train hurtling
thru the intestines of the city.
i'm reading *African Religions & Philosophy.*
the man next to me is buried in the news,
(Rhodesia is arguing with Zimbabwe for the headlines.)
reality is spitting in the face of reality.

at the far end of the car—a black man,
severed from his sanity so suddenly
he still wears a tie & shined shoes.
he is enraged, battering on mostly
                    at the tunnel we pass thru.

"why yall following me! i'll get you ! i'll get you!"
he is mind of my mind.   even now
i can hear the good doctor calling the guards
to lead me away, my fist clinched at my side
wanting to smash his glasses & make him see.

THE ATTENDANTS TO MEMORY LAPSE

i remember
he thought to himself
as a helper.
who was he fooling? —
his function
to make my life
a practical joke—
"you don't like our little hotel?"
time & time again they said it,
hiding my poetry books, prowling my correspondence,
lying about meanings to remembered friends.
my world, a cigar box full of letters,
a shirt with cigarette burns,
handed down from patient to patient
                    like smallpox.

i remember friends
insisting that i wasn't crazy,
writing to me about Mingus, about Monk.

i remember
rocking, rocking
'till anger became a flood
                    directed
towards his white face,
his white uniform,
where the keys to my life
dangled from a beltstrap.

i remember the patients telling me
"yeah, you hit him, hit him good."
i do remember that they said so.

i remember waking
strapped again to the Lazarus bed.

DID THEY HELP ME AT THE STATE
HOSPITAL FOR THE CRIMINALLY INSANE?

For this one
You need a pocket dictionary
That enters biblical charity
As a synonym for atrocities
Committed in a silent
Partner's best interest.
Cleave end & mean,
Wall them, pin them
In antagonistic corners,
Departmentalize, dissect them
'Til the sense in such nonsense
Is twisted loose, Say "normal"
By all means, by any means
Is correct, justified.
Don't question this!
Declare a holy war on madness,
But stay unmoved by it all like god,
Keep the goal aloft.
& if the goal is missed,
A fraction too long
On the electroshock machine,
A little too much Haldol,
Be quick & resolute with disclaimer.

Then i suppose things could be compared.
Did Truman help the Japs?
By saving countless Kamikazes
From thoughtless death?
Did Hitler help the Jews?
With Jewish enterprise?
Sticktogetherness?
At least the bathwater
Finds its way home to sea.
So when the baby

Who was thrown out with it
Grows up despite all odds
Having drunk his fill
Of castor-oil reality
& held it on his stomach,
Commend the state's parental guidance,
Shake its rank statutory hand.
The state has made a man.

Yeah, they helped me.

INSANITY AS STYLE

start out with suspenders, sunglasses
                             & a beard,
see how far they'll let you go with it,
blow your nose a lot,
stuff your handkerchief
                         into your front
pants pocket, decide to eat only potato
chips for breakfast, look four times each way
before you cross the street, salute
every flag you see, ride a lawn mower
                                to work,
converse with people seriously
                   about the aesthetics of polka dots,
carry cheap wine in a peanut butter jar
in your Gucci briefcase, don't brush your teeth,
say you make your living writing poems.

when they come get you
be sure to put up a fight.

TO THE X FUNCTION OF Y

another one went down.
a record 103 are dead.
they'll call back
at tricky wrench this time
& shuffle an extra man into line.
the bank will issue more policies.
someone will get the new coffee pot
with defective handle
for a small opening balance.

someone who expected accuracy
in the screws, more room
to move around inside the thing
will be ejected from his swivel chair.
someone will say, "I have no knowledge
of the aforementioned occurrences,
nor do I have any understanding of how
the said occurrences relate to myself
and Mr. Winecroft."

someone else will check the spelling of "technology"
in the dictionary.
someone's ballpoint pen will be out of ink.
                and
as always, a few reputable men in the encyclopedia
whose thinking seemed so well-grounded
just a few years back
will fade into the graveyard
                        of time.

TSIT/ AS PARALLEL
(for Lee)
(in the wake of the Andrew Young situation)

a Yiddish word
—a jerk, a pull
at the heart—

centuries of touch,
the slow grind of civilization,
from there to now—
a circle,
perhaps your grandfather
buying a rotten head of lettuce
at a sidewalk stand.

& she, selling bagels
from a steaming cart
in December cold.

ten cents she wants to feed her children, she says
in an accent i don't understand.

fresh from Mississippi,
i have a nickel,
she takes it, fumbles inside her ragged coat.

this—
the panorama of Hitler
in the backroom of a bar
huddled with several others in low voice—
Europe is wondering again
whether a Jew hath eyes.

so many   how many?
5 million, ten million?
only the first death mattered, says the poet,
so true and such a lie.

my flesh goes out and goes out
until it contradicts itself
and hardens at the bone.
No, we never will get it all told,
this human story, so willful, everywhere so entwined.

Look at Asia—Hiroshima
glance at Europe,
glance the other way—
50 million Africans dead
in the crossing of the Atlantic
yanking every ideal at the heart.
& those "starving masses" of Latin America,
everywhere the screams, the silent weeping yanking us
down, down into the benthos of the sea.

THE WORD "NIGGER"

it's a good word
to describe a few crap shooters
standing in front of the pool hall
passing a bottle, a good word
for old men, all their lives
opening doors for every white man
who needs to enter a bank,
a good word for a Saturday night murder
& if driven deep enough into the skull
one becomes a monkey in a tree in Africa
but then becomes the tree itself
                              as magic & as study.

i'm sure the first ones,
despair so deep, as to leap overboard
never thought they'd get a word
into the dictionary, and to think
we made them take it out.
they'd be proud of us.

THRU THE EYES OF THE YOUNG MAN
IN THE VIDEO GAME PARLOR

at first Christ on the cross
then only the cross
where limbs abstracted
became 2 intersecting lines
stretching forever as perpendiculars
then only the point of intersection
& the small dot, the planet earth,
at the point of intersection, the point
where the eyes of the young man in conflict
disappear into the point.
he is coming home,
home to us.
bless you mother
bless you father
bless you PAC MAN
bless the eye
bless you DEFENDER
& ZAXXON of the dilated iris
bless you TEMPEST of the iris
CENTIPEDE of the pupil
& bless you war, war,
the vision of war,
the dream of war,
the image of war,
before the act of war,
the machines of war
& the idea of war growing, growing
way-out of proportion.
bless you skinny kid
way out skinny kid
who is cleansed in the flowing blood
& the murdered eye.

ADOPTION
for C

i come again & again to this
like a signpost driven
into the concrete of my memory—
you standing there
on the avenue of americas, crying,
my seed bulging in your stomach,
the rain splattering everything
but never washing us clean.
it's a sore in the landscape of my images,
a teen love novel that i can never write,
the summer romance that ended with a flat tire.
that was the summer economics became
real to me. that was a lot to winter—
jesus born & given over to the social agencies.

he had the cutest little egg-shaped head.

SUFFER THE CHILDREN

you will find my fragments on every street corner
where a neon sign blinks the surreal image
of scotches and sex larger than sunrise.
in every marijuana dream you will find drugged pieces
of me dribbling off the end of a four-four tune
into the void. you will see me in greetings
& be unfulfilled by my salutation in the smokey
rooms of thought. in each shard reflecting light
from the broken church window you will find
the taper of my lament waving, indomitable & green.
& when the pieces of your living memory stick to you
like lint on the priest's black coat you will find
your Gestalt in the eye of my pen & yes the inundating
small lyrics of two minute commercials booming
out the economy will drive you back into the breath
from my nostrils. & i will smile & speak your name
& not forget you at the end of the long block
without your weapon. No, i'll be running circle
round you like a halo. i'll be there too when the question
is posed about the stirring in the woodwork
that could never be a rat. & when the preacher
gets into his luxury car & drives away
i will not chastise you. i am in the butterflies
& the lion, hating every cage & cubicle that chain you.
in the tremor of my speech will be the hesitancy
of your courage. in my madness will be your redemption.
you will live in me without the hypnosis
of your mother's garments. you will drink my energy
with temperance & grow to tolerate the urges of my anger.

ARTAUD & I

he is certainly as right
as i will grant any man, half right,
rambling, raging against
the mad analyst mind
down thru the centuries
who with stolen anus
in his pocket
would mold to us to some form
more than we are already,
a thing of clanks and metal functions.
they're full of shit,
their eloquent profanities,
nothing more these emissaries,
ambassadors of shit.

Artaud knew them ultimately
as the sniff-arounds, they are, himself,
but much more, mostly them.

what you could call our problem
is how to say it—Artaud's rambling,
his rage, what else is there?
when you total up the lies,
what more than murder?

think about it, nine holes
with which to feel the clean blue sky
they have secreted in noxious gas.

only mad laughter, locks & red lights
we wanted to be exits.

MEDITATION

"Sit," he said
"i won't bore you with the stories.
the long & then the short of it
is that all the wisdom of others
is the wisdom of others,
is simply noise.
there are stories, there are stories,
but the story is the sitting.
a thousand stories fly out from you—Sit.

Sit, i will tell the story of the sitting
without strong drink or dancing
we will turn the music down.

we will sit.

we will live.
we will die.

but
we will sit."

       2

from the straightback chair
i am intent on the Ethiopian painting
on my wall.
      i can't make out the Amharic
of the white men & black men
who look at each other with mean-comic eyes
as they row down the Nile.
it means everything.

it means nothing, those strange animals
                    in the water,
those swords like the leaves of trees,
those harnessed cows, unnaturally monstrous.

             3

a leg, a leg,
an arm, an arm

da doom doom
da doom doom
da doom doom
da doom doom
da doom doom
da doom doom
da doom doom

now, let it go.
just let it go.

POEM FOR ANYONE WHO MIGHT SURVIVE
THE NUCLEAR WAR & FALLOUT TO FIND THIS
IF BY CHANCE IT MIGHT SURVIVE

i tt
    claaimmeed it   di dn't   thhhen
claimmmmmed
               the   disclaimer
   of it,   then   disclaimed itt again,

      saying   nevvvvvvvvvvvvveeeeeerrrrrr

until   ffffffinalllly   faaaaacccedddddddddddd
wwwwwwwwwwwwwwiiiiiiiiiith
        rocksrocksrocksrocksrocksrocksrocks
cccclllaaaaiiiimmm   mmm
   iiiiiiiiiiiiinnnnnnnnnnnnnnnggggggggg
each   otherrr's   ccccllaaiimms

   thhtthhaaat   iiiitttt   dddiiiiidddnn't
        do   it
nnnnnoooorr   d:diddddd   aaaaannnnnyyy
of its   aaaaaggggents.

TO ASSEMBLE AN ARMY FOR YOUR CAUSE

Concoct a ceremony as a test of truth.

> put a key on a string
> & hide it in any book,
> turn to your page
> each time they don't agree with you,
> take out the key,
> quote your passage,
> hold the key steady in your hand,
> tell them it's a god,
> Marx or Jesus, that moves the key
> every time they lie.
> say it's not you lying
> & not unnerving gall
> of your nervy fingers.
> throw in a few old bones,
> a few universal guilts,
> curse their hair, the color of their eyes,
> add a dream, make up a diet, draw a moon,
> a swastika, an ankh,
> flip the pages, read again,
> xerox this & pass it out on the streets.

soon enough a few vague souls will stumble forward,
be sure to quote your passage,
mumble a few throaty words.

you'll get your motley crew.

WHAT I'M TALKING ABOUT

what I am talking about
is that "Mars is our nearest neighbor,"
that the sun is *only* 93,000,000 miles away.
what I'm talking about is our farthest neighbor,
what I'm talking about is only and lonely,
is the paintings of Hieronymous Bosch,
the glowing eyes of the night forest in my mind,
the scaly green things the third eye glimpses
darting into the underbrush.

I'm talking about all those African sculptures
that are a fish, a man, and a bird with horns.

I'm talking about that salt sea smell
I can almost taste
when they say the word "life."

I'm talking about that sea
that is gathering its dance in your eyes, that sea
that you can almost see
when you look at your own face
in a convex mirror, that sea and its salt,
that sea salt that comes rolling
down your cheeks
to make you human.
and you cry like a baby
you cry, baby, you cry.

AIR BAG FAILS TO SAVE MAN
FROM SUICIDE
(in his memory)
June 1981

"A man jumped from the 19th floor
of a housing project and landed
on an emergency air bag, but he died
several hours later, police said."

thus the article begins,
in fact has come to be, ordinary
for we are living in what the philosophers call
"the modern world."

Walter Foster, 20 year old black man,
shown in two photographs—
in the first, he stands threatening, poised
on a ledge,
a cop nearby, gesturing,
full of emptiness.

the second shows the young man
sailing past a window headlong,
arms extended, fist balled,
like an inverted superman.

he has on a T-shirt,
a fashionable pair of jeans,
appears to be shoeless,
no doubt one of the 7% unemployed,
if you're black, his age,
15 to 65% depending on who's quoting the stats.
everything is debatable.
a man is dead from ifs and buts.

2

i wonder had he ever heard that song?
who was it? THE COMMODORES?
THE IMPRESSSIONS? FOUR TOPS? TEMPTATIONS?
"In the ghetto only the strong survive,"
the base line pounding a steady monotonous beat.

i wonder did he see that track meet
where the long distance runner
turned philosophical and breathing hard
into the microphone said,
"It's a good life if you don't tire."

i'm sure he wouldn't have read *The Wild Duck*.

3

this is America,
purple mountains' majesty,

the flat plains of Kansas,
The World Trade Center,

this is planet earth,
a small ball spinning, spinning.

you are alone.
don't pretend you don't understand.

SUICIDE POEM

i should give it up—
this getting up to try,
the trying to get up for it.
but i've been black so long
i've lost my curiousity about dark unknowns
or should i say i still have it?

should i say—life?
simply tomorrow's misery
stacked on top of today's.

so,
should i become a wino
& drool about a dime?
should i sleep in hallways
& eat canned heat in the winter?
live from pneumonia to pneumonia?
should i quit getting paranoid
in front of the landlord?
get the police to find me a home?
better still, just check it in, check it in,
tell god & the devil,
"yall ain't responsible for me,"
say, "i'm coming to you pale jesus,"
                              & give it up.
but
who would be left
to condemn religion,
to dream of a beserk Idi Amin
returned this time with atomic power?
who would be left to be afraid of mysteries?
to look into the eyes of women?
to approve the reverence of life?
who would be around to die trying?

SPLITS

a drop of blood, a single sperm,
a piece of lint for a thought,
a speck of falling star
trapped in gray matter & synapse, in the muscles,
where the endless galaxies
of mind & body fly apart
in disease & breathless loss.
hard facts, the bits of sand,
we call our selves,
& separate, aloof,
little elves that dance & die—
will is all we've ever had—
to unify, to integrate,
to make the highest art of this
would-be religion.
to know each song trailing off
like flecks of windblown dust,
stupid dust without metaphor,
dust without redemption,
to see each atom sheared of its beard, that,
i am afraid, is glory,
more like the truth,
more like the science of our endings.

THE SILENT COUDS

my spare little apartment, the clothes should be hung up,
the books arranged, the desk with its clutter of papers
should be straightened. A spare life should be just that,
honed to its purpose. The Buddhist says that death
is so certain that we should live as though we are already dead.
And so I write these words for you, my friend, words written
many, many years from now are written now by a man who lived
many, many years ago. A man whom death vacuumed away like
carpet dust
has written on a blank piece of paper that you and he are specks
of the farthest star, that you and he are the stuff of the silent
clouds.

PROPHECY

something bizarre in the clouds
something down river in the rapids
the trees strangely still
the world on the window ledge
                    about to leap.

WHAT WOULD GIVE MEANING

what would give meaning
to the slow swirl
of light and darkness
that settles around me before I sleep,
that swirl that sometimes keeps me awake?

what would give meaning
to the unprecedented fact of being alive
with only words and my finger pointed
at the graceful dance of the Milky Way,
with only words to say—
it is so truly a miracle.

& i am afraid, so terribly afraid
that God, for instance, is only a word,
that death, for instance, is a red brick,
that death, for instance, is a sleek gray cat,
that springs into the lap & licks us in the face.

MYSTERIOSO
(after Thelonious Monk)

thru the neon window,
a large fluorescent Pabst beer sign,
the flicker of a diamond ring in the mirror,
a glass, another,
a flash of fire,
red cigarette ends, smoke.

i remember when we needed them,
even the one in the wig
        perched on the high stool near the door,
even the guy in the yellow suit
        & lizard shoes.

tonight, though,
i need only you,
only you, my curious reader, you
with your desire touching mine
like a child's nose on a cool window;
a distant soul to love these words,
their thin dangerous music
scented with the incense of narrow city streets
& the moonlight's pocket change,
these words perfumed by streetlights,
nylon stockings & the plastic seats of taxis
on the wet avenues, these words
that are a mustache for the moon
& the lipstick of lady death.

BAD LUCK LYRIC

since, in fact,
ain't nothing I can do
to turn life back
I go on
walking under ladders
& the furious stars,
go on with black cats
crossing my path,
go on making these weird markings
in the dust.
old man laughed
cause he was riding in the saddle
when moma's belly bulged
she knew she'd lost another battle
& here I come spinning into the world
like a lemon, a cherry & a plum.

WHITMAN'S BODY ELECTRIC

i have the urge of stars tonight
to be beyond act/react
& politics pursuant
to this statute or that state.

tonight, i have the urge of stars,
a clear straight urge
devoid of words that lock like shackles
& all that shackles will not free.

i have the urge of stars tonight,
to wait a billion years for nothing
to become its something else,
its something else not body   not mind.

THE DIVINE ANIMALS
CHICAGO YMCA WINDOW #1139
June 1982

i am in love with windows
& the unpainted city thru them,
the crane with wrecking ball
as the El moves above the buildings
along its tracks.
so easily i imagine
all of this as darkness
Zinjanthropus eaten bones & all,
a passing thought before the sperm
took form, the first slithering frog
hopping a few feet onto land,
his nervous system freezing.
so easily i imagine myself drowning,
the water coming up to meet me like concrete
but then i surface & am shimmering
& wet with living,
the world forever unknown
that I have been.

STATE & MIND
OR   1980, DECEMBER
STATE OF MIND

you will find no open-ended questions
          in me,   this time,
too close to answers,
the world now at the edge of finale,
the hint of persona, only for you
who live in me, only the mask,
no glance sideways,
nothing so assertive as a period;
i wait—
whether spring rain, winter storm,
the beginning, end of summer, the end,
i have no clue—
how long, o' how long,
even that dangerous, more so now,
too loud like numbers on a social security card—
if i knew a way other than poetry to speak to you,
i would signal with matches in the dark,
beckon for you to follow,
not even metaphor would disturb
those few trees along the avenue—
i whisper, i embrace you,
we always wanting life,
always wanting what we want now.
i am disappearing now,
here, at the crossroads,
this dilemma, flight,
this dilemma—a coming out party
with our hands up.
we will, i hope, meet again. . .

THE AMNESIA OF SETTING

A star
        further
than the one
you thought the farthest
                    star
an existence
beyond the farthest existence
you have imagined,
a self
so many selves removed from this self
that if it came to you
whispering in a spring breeze,
if it came as a blade of grass,
as a ray of sunlight
or as a star further
than the farthest star,
if it came to you
as the perfect elegance of a circle,
as the eye of the pyramid,
if it came as a torrential rain,
if it said, "Hello, how's the family?"
if it called your name in a bank
or bought you a drink in a bar,
if it said, "Let's get together
and have lunch sometime,"
if it greeted you—"Long time,
no see, man,"
or phoned to remind you
of the class reunion.   suppose
it called you "nigger,"
or whizzed by in a souped-up Ford
and gave you a "fuck you"
with its middle finger—
you would surely say, "Where from?",

would try to remember
who you were and they and it
and what it was they thought you were
and what you thought of them
back then when you were a different matter
that can never be created or destroyed.

'SUGAR BLUES'

"I'll buy a huge piece of meat, cook it up for dinner,
and then right before it's done, I'll break down
and have what I wanted for dinner in the first place—
bread and jam . . . all I ever really want is sugar."
                                                    Andy Warhol

if you start out here,
you get soup cans,
american flags on the flattest surface,
you get red, white & blue.

you ain't white,
don't make no difference if you red,
you gon' be blue.

i was born a child of the blues,
long songs whispering thru the cotton fields,
mothers raped, children sucking
on whatever the master threw out,
John in the big house going mad
for ways to poison them.

if you start out here
you must go down, deep down,
to the grid of the eyes,
to the inner ear to find yourself,
you must go down to the killing floor,
go down to spirituals
& the north star beckoning
as only a faint glint in your mind.

if you start out here
you like the old man said,
"been down so long,

rising ain't even crossed my mind."

down here,
we go down & lift up the world,
from a cane field, from the hold of a ship.

PARTY OR WE'VE ARRIVED AT WHAT?

a gathering of art ideas
they stalked each other,
circled, countered, countercircled,
           split   reassembled,
i'd be prone to call it dancing.
at midnight they crystallized,
became contemporary conviviality.
some would go home with others,
make love or sodomy.

socialism & madness jeered from opposite corners.
the others called them too intense.
the one lacked compassion & freedom,
the other had too much or vice versa.
astrology & numerology paraded about,
antique clothes & all, teetering like teenage girls
at the edges of circles, flashing like stars
to the center of attention; they galled science.
they inadvertently flirted with anarchy
who came in cowboy boots & thrust its thumbs
into the beltstraps of its levis & drank too much.
ideologies & mysticisms came in hoards.
born-again christianity was just so happy
it'd been invited. it told all its past sins
& hogged the marijuana, its new one.
existentialism went on & on
in a small tight conversation,
its chief proponent, despairing individualism,
drunk & furious because socialism was there.
capitalism was dressed for the occasion
& pouring whiskey down everybody's throat.
it'd given the affair & considered
all the other ideas bums, interesting,
but still bums. it had big awkward hands
                        & chainsmoked.

ALMOST A LYRIC
(for Lee)

it is indeed the world
outside your bedroom window
& my words in that world are imminent—
Europe is a word as is Africa
as is black as is white.

understand   i didn't create these words.
the world fed them to me until i accepted blackness
& wrapped it around me, shimmering shroud that it is.
as a child my eyes drank it in, it became a longing
mysterious to be shed of it / to pass into a world
of ice cream and cola, grassy lawns, the shit i flee now
until it ties me in a knot.   this skin will not come
loose from Europe or Africa without a man inside
coming loose from half the stuff that he's made from.

we are more real than i'd expected.
i am witness. we don't come loose easily,
an obelisk of human kind, legs and arms entwined
up & up & up—not even god is watching us,
but we are watching ourselves, until the singing
is a fettered voice, unraveling in rage,
                                    rejoicing in a cage.

until we are mired in circumstance,
our feelings reduced to social science studies,
until we are butterflies in a jar.

still this poem is tribute to possibility,
almost a lyric, this song of the bees in the rose.
i give you words. be careful, they will sting—
like the twist of worlds unfolding & the irony
of black/white love.

SCARS

almost
casually
now
i discover on my wrists
one welt-like scar,
two, like burns.
the first
from when i would have killed
a white boy
trying to slash open
an order
thick with injustice
like cheesecake,
rich with it.
i thought it vulnerable,
thought being young
i could cut its throat.
it was a form of suicide
& a form of surgery, personal & social.

the other two scars
are the mark of handcuffs & of law,
tightened close to the bone.

not symbolic scars,
but literal,
a branding, the law's signature.

in our ways, we,
both the law & i, were right.
for hurt is insolent;
it strikes out.
the ways of law
a steadfast vice,

flypaper for the little things
that brush against it.

law would have us think it high principle
that governs us, that gods & ethics
hold & protect us perfectly.
but i have walked these city streets
& known, being black, that nothing
keeps the traps of justice from summarily
snapping & ensnaring me
except the firm way i've learned to wait
& write the rage away.

FILLING UP BLACK HOLES

it works as a literal conspiracy,
the counter-espionage communication bureau
of the forgotten church in the wilderness,
of the look in the elevator,
the notecards & pen in his pocket
& why her smile,
& why so many beers last night
& why always the why
of the picture from the 1950s,
the movie where she turns to face him
with a cigarette in her mouth,
the ring on his finger, the telephone click,
& why were her legs crossed that way,
why the letter from California.
any act or image will do to fill us up,
all of them will do, all leaping
along spongy gray matter
driven by a drum of blood.

VISION

they quote Marx
like the Bible,
quote the Bible,
like Marx ain't the god of the realm
& i get leery
but will not sit & gaze
at the candle's shadow on the wall.
no, i heat up, wax rage.
yet sometimes what i see & don't see—
both illusions striving to be real—
the visions—blood & gore,
picture-perfect paradise, no blood or gore—
both alien to this planet/
probably unknowable/certainly unknown—
only found in books, words
like poetry in the eyes of a vision maimed
in the streets—
do i comment on the deep, sweet curiosity
of a child's eyes in his severed head?
the world—hard choices,
Nina Simone's sad voice in the wee hours,
"what difference does it make which one i choose,
either way i lose."

THE STATUE OF LIBERTY

since i'd never been inside the lady
i took the trip by ferry
& took my son,
to introduce him
to the moldy mist
settled on most precious things,
to tell him how this came to be
& how now the way's all green & tarnished
& why it cost ten cents to view it all from shore
& why one gets all he'll ever get for a dime ride
up thru the stone base of liberty
to the stairs that are the real bitch.

we'd only gone a few flights up
the curving iron cold stairs
when he complained of tiredness.

i think he got the message,
the message huddled poor there
on the staircase where the elevator stopped
& slid back down to the ground.

WEAPONS

("you've chosen your weapon, man")
Ron Welburn

i am thinking of my son
playing with the 49¢ puzzle map of america.
thinking of a junky
walking along the upper east side of manhattan,
these capitals of grain & beef,
those arsenals & energy plants
outside denver or dallas or raleigh,
those centers of steel & commerce,
that junky in rockefeller's neighborhood.

i am thinking of Burroughs-
how he throws the pieces up,
how they all come down together,
arrayed in uniforms, in bed together,
how the pieces fall into my hands,
a naked lunch, a machine gun, a hypodermic needle,
a chicken, an egg, a pair of eyes ground up in salami
anything could hit me, anything could fall
            into "the wrong hands."
even a poem could waylay some governor,
some banker, some pig doing his gig.

SPONTANEOUS JAZZ PIECE

It is my mother,
how without writing it down,
she lived it, over the mouth
of hell & walked that walk
and talked that talk
& told it like it was,
how blues rose up classical
in her soul, how in the middle
of morning she coached away
my nightmares, how day is not
day without her, and night,
spontaneous as good morning,
good morning, say good morning.
be a man, stand tall, stand tall.
Tall men coming on from Dunbar
Lias, Lias, bless the Lord.
Don't, you know tha' day's abroad,
Dance & Sing, Dance & Sing.

THE MEASURED RAGE:
A POETIC STATEMENT FOR THE PRINTER

i want to be even
like the justified line
      so justified
that when the end comes
it doesn't slop over with rage
i want to be neat
left   right left combinations
        clean, crafted menace
           measured anger
that doesn't overkill.
i want to dispose of things
with justification & diplomacy
i want to hate & keep my sportscoat on
i want to be a steel will in-the-infighting of the line
                type of poet
said precisely i want to get even
    precisely   even.

MAKING POEMS

let's be done
with all their notations of inspiration,
done with all their notions
of poets sipping tea,
waiting ever so sweetly
on the muses to sail by.
let's be done with polite art.
i'll say it straightout—
i vomited the damn things up
from the bottom of the world
because i had to or go mad.
then i went again to make something of the mess.
i never called them 'poems'
until you did.